To Becmag

FROM OFFICE CHAIR
TO DECK CHAIR
HOW TO HAVE 2 SUMMERS A YEAR

Thank you for also empowering others to fulfil on their dreams

Best of luck

Peter Jordan

PETER SAUNDERS

FROM OFFICE CHAIR TO DECK CHAIR

Published by
10-10-10 Publishing
1-9225 Leslie St.
Richmond Hill
Ontario, Canada
L4B 3H6

ISBN:9781517137298

For information about special discounts for bulk purchases,
please contact 10-10-10 Publishing at 1-888-504-6257

Printed in the United States of America

Contents

Acknowledgements

I would like to express my thanks to Vishal Morjaria and Naval Kumar for finally landing this idea and editing the book.

My family have always allowed for my eccentric/adventurous personality , and granted me freedom to travel and planted the seeds for so many things.

None of this would have been possible without so many people here in London in Brazil, and upon courses and mentorship along the way.

Thanks to so many people who have contributed, often without knowing and thanks to the journey and ability to travel.

To my family who showed me from a young age the value of travel, and set me with a good foundation to explore and make friends.

And finally to you, for taking the step on an adventure which can only be yours.

Foreword

Have you ever looked out on your life and wished it were different? Did you have plans to visit different countries, and either did this just once on a tour, or put this aside as something to only consider once you were retired?

Many years ago, the seeds were planted to consider being able to live a summer during the winter months in the UK. However, this all seemed like a distant dream, or only something for a chosen few lucky people in society...

Peter is someone who has been living like this since 2003. It had been brewing a long time, and then finally someone asked him: "How do you manage to do this every year?" This has become a way of life now for over a decade.

Sometimes a question can turn the course of our lives. This one brought to light something that was not only available to him, but that could be shared so that more people could participate. So began many years of living in the sun during the winter season of the UK. Once started, it is very difficult to turn back and spend a winter in the dark and rain. A mix of training, doing and personal development and mentoring has allowed Peter to develop a lifestyle that through sharing can now be accessible to many others.

Raymond Aaron
Leading Transformational Success Mentor
New York Times Best-Selling Author

Chapter 1
Introduction

I have been living in London and Brazil since 2003. For me it occurred initially as an adventure and the fulfilment of a dream... Where did this all start? One holiday in the Caribbean in 1980. It was the stark contrast of experiencing sunshine during December and into the New Year, and returning to university in January in the freezing cold and snow.

My fellow Engineering student at The Queen's College Oxford also went away to Australia, and both of us returned vital and healthy, instead of our pasty-faced friends who had made it through the English winter. (He later ended up on the board of a FTSE-100 company, so maybe it should be part of the curriculum?)

That set the seed: Can I do this myself in future? But how? How can I do this when I have graduated? How can people do this with their families? Is it possible to do this without being a millionaire? How much do I need to earn to live this lifestyle?

However, as life took over, the commitment to engineering and investment banking seemed to put the dream further and further away. And then one day, through luck and judgement, having set up my life to pay me, I made the decision to go to Brazil for the winter.

That has been my life since 2003. It is hard to describe the benefits, but here are just a few: Well-being, energy, being more healthy and happy, and getting to live with vitality for the 2-3 months of winter, which were normally my hibernation months.

When I shared this way of life with a friend, she commented: "I have met a few people who have done that once in their life, and travel around, but how is it that you have done it EVERY year, for the past few years?"

For me, it had become normal. Yes, a few fortunate circumstances conspired to make this available to me. Then I decided to answer that question: How can I make that more available to others like YOU, from where YOU stand in YOUR life?

Each time I have travelled it has been fun, and it would be so much fun to have this available to other people, like you. Occasionally people come out to Brazil for a few days, and get to see this. Sometimes, they stay for a bit longer, and sometimes they too have stayed for a few months.

I love meeting people on my travels, and more recently, I also love to return home and appreciate the life I lead when I get back to the UK. At times, I have no idea why more people do not take this on. Sometimes people may have the money but not the time, or the time but not the money; and sometimes it may be another hidden factor...

My mission is to make this available in a way that can impact your life. You may not do exactly what I have done in Brazil and Rio de Janeiro, but it may spark something inside of you to be able to bring your own version of your dreams into reality.

May this be the first step into bringing that into existence for you.

Further information on my website:
www.FromOfficeChairToDeckChair.com

What Most People Do

Most people fall into 1 of 2 categories:

Category 1 - People are so caught up in their own lives and bills that they give up on their dream. No more nurturing of the dream, just finishing there, and continuing with their life and career, as it takes them.

Category 2 - People who begin to plan, then do more planning, and then more planning, until it spills over into next week, next month, or even next year. And then again, it gets set aside.

Do you fall into the category of putting other things first, because you think it would take SUCH a lot of effort, or being financially independent? Or you might wonder if your boss would allow you to take 3, 6 or 9 months off. All sorts of reasons might creep in. Do you live your life within the decisions made by other people, and forget to make your own way in life?

As humans, I would assert that we thrive and come alive when we take life on – if only a little bit. And today, we live in times when that is so much more accessible.

From my perspective, it is almost as if people decide FIRST that it is difficult to do, and then cite all the evidence to me. I should be in London – my career does not allow for that. Really? Do you use the phone – do you use skype? Do you physically HAVE to be in your home city? All the time?

If you are able to work from home, or away from the office, maybe this is within your reach.

I have met people who are busy, very successful financially, but with almost no freedom to move or live where they wish. They may be stuck within 20 minutes of a hospital, as they are a key part of a team in emergencies. This is rare, but we live now, with the decisions that we made in our yesterdays.

On these travels, I have met students, people studying for Masters degrees and PhDs, people working as chefs in a bar, teaching English as a 2nd language. Working as a medic, a specialist.

Back in London, some of the most successful people I know are free and financially solvent. Yet, out of habit they spend their winters around the UK. That is okay. However , if you have once tried a warm holiday during winter time in your part of the world, the contrast is very appealing.

Most people get stuck in the habits of their friends or family and copy them. Now we are entering a golden age of travel, where it is possible to visit almost anywhere, at a fraction of the costs it would have been 15-35 years ago.

Finally, the internet opens up all sorts of opportunities. The first space to gain freedom is in the space between our ears – in our own mind.

Where would you travel to, if money were no object?

_____
_____
_____
_____

Avoiding Pitfalls

Be sure to avoid pitfalls

What do these look like?

Ask yourself what stops you from trying out something new. Pitfalls are assuming several things:

1. It costs so much
2. If I try it and it goes wrong then my life is over
3. I have been doing Job X , so far, so if I go abroad I HAVE to work in that field
4. I do not speak the language
5. Any other variation, where we tell ourselves it is so difficult, that we look for evidence that supports that assumption

The other pitfalls depend on the conversations we have with people. Are we speaking to people who have done this, or to people who have never tried it? Are we focusing on what works, or on what may go wrong?

Notice this; think of the most successful company, or place, and google it. Then add in a dangerous word, and you will get all sorts of horror stories. Do the reverse, and see what happens.

Try this with a friend:

Sit them in a room and ask them to make a note mentally of anything in the room , of a certain prominent colour (for that room) e.g. blue. Give them a minute. Then ask them to close their eyes. Then ask them to recall anything in the room , of another colour (several objects in that colour) which is not blue, say red, or green.

Notice how few objects they can recall (with eyes closed) of that colour red, say. Then ask them to open up their eyes and point out how many. If they have named a few, well done. Normally, we instruct our brain to notice what we command it to se. In this case, the colour blue.

This applies so much into people, objects, ideas. Whatever questions we ask will allow us to notice different answers.

It may therefore be useful to ask: How can I make this work? What do I need to know? Keep on asking this of people, who can tell you FROM THEIR OWN EXPERIENCE . Second-hand experience is also valid, but it helps to speak to people who have been there, done it, and got the t-shirt, so to speak.

Who could you speak to now, and what would be empowering questions?

Speak to: _____

Questions: _____

_____

_____

See some powerful questions at:
www.FromOfficeChairToDeckChair.com

Living the Dream

So what does living the dream really look like? At first it is great fun, everything and everyone is new, there are no rules, it is like living in discovery. And part of it is remembering what it is that we leave behind, and appreciate that we have a choice in any moment.

Live your dream. No copies.

At times, living the dream means stepping into the unknown. A chance meeting, an entrance into a language school. A visit to a family home, or being around people who value you.

It may not always look easy at first, but coming out the other side, I got to have a sense of who I was beyond the network of people I knew back in the UK. Living the dream is not always predictable.

Joy and dreams come from unexpected places.

It may be exploring, finding out stories, or following your instinct in far-off places. For instance, I was in the Amazon Jungle, and met some local native indians indigenous to the Amazon. When asked if I had any questions, I asked them about any stories they had in their own culture, any myths or folk tales. The lady was about 50, with a teenager cooking fish over a fire. She began to tell me the story of the Guarana tree. It was fascinating.

When I got back to Rio de Janeiro, I shared this with several friends from Rio (Cariocas, as they are known). None of them had heard of this story. Guarana is a national drink, - a bit like a healthy drink, which can also served in a can. So, we can find value and humanity anywhere.

Our dreams, may not be revealed where we think.

Living your dream when travelling may also involve places, but remember it can also involve people and the local wildlife.

Part of living a dream was often being in a place to be of contribution, and connected to people. Find your own expression of this. As much as visiting great places is amazing, it could be visiting people in their homes, however grand or simple. It could also be giving people a free treatment or sharing some of your knowledge, or taking extra food from lunch or dinner, and sharing it with a homeless person on the street. Do this via a local, so there are no misunderstandings.

A beer, a song on the beach; it is worth finding out what locals do. And remember they do love hearing about your own culture.

What does your dream look like?

_____

_____

_____

_____

See dream tips on:
www.FromOfficeChairToDeckChair.com

How Long This Dream Took to Fulfil

This may not just happen overnight. Looking back, it took several years, and a slice of luck to be in a position to travel. You may need to save up, or set up something to work online back in your home country to cover your costs.

Even so, it took several visits to meet people, and find out different ways to sort out accommodation. There are a variety of options: flats, apartments, hotels, hostels, and people who may host you or rent out rooms. The choice depends on your budget and requirements, of sharing and privacy.

My dream started in 1980 or so, but it took until 2003 to act on it. That was not what you call lightning quick. However, once started, it was much easier to repeat it the following year. Each year, I developed contacts, and more knowledge and a changing appreciation of what I liked to do.

Back in London, I found many activities that linked into what I did in Brazil, with music and dancing and people. This opened up options to visit when I returned. Then I looked to what could be available if I invested.

So, this is an evolving dream. I have to remember to check on what my dream is now, as opposed to just going there, because I had a dream 20-30 years ago. Life and dreams do evolve. I am not sure about you, but I can get stuck in decisions I made a long time ago – as opposed to reviewing my dreams.

What were your dreams 5, 10 years ago, and what dreams could you have now?

Dreams as a kid

_____

Dreams 5-10 years ago

_____

Dreams today

_____

_____

Once I began to tick off items, I could become more independent. Could I be in each country 6 months a year? Even now there is more to be done to have a permanent visa or visiting visa beyond 3 months. As life stands, you decide what works for you in each country.

Also after a month, there is a different rhythm to fulfil on the dream. I look back, and if I had not moved out of investment banking into property, I would not have had this freedom to travel as I can now. Yes, you can get posted by your work to another country, but that is not in your control. It can be convenient, but again, it is your employer that decides. If it works for you, it can be great, as they deal with all the bureaucracy and help with paperwork, bank accounts, accommodation etc.

See tips on goals setting on:
www.FromOfficeChairToDeckChair.com

So Thinking of You — Why Now?

Look at what would work for you, in this time, to be able to take this on. For me, it just seemed to happen. I had split from my Brazilian girlfriend, and yet had this idea in my head. I was single, and no commitments, so if not now, when would it be so easy?

Life opened up when I made the commitment. Within a few weeks of buying the ticket, I met Brazilians in coffee shops, at a demonstration I made at a music school, and at breakfast meetings. Prior to that year I had never met a Brazilian in London. Incidentally, after I returned from Brazil for the first time, they had a huge month of Brazil at Selfridges, one of the largest stores in central London. It was as if Brazil had followed me back on the plane!

So, sometimes making a decision allows the universe to open up ways to make it work. It is also a great exercise to make things happen. When we take a holiday or a trip, we enter a different way of being in life. Call it holiday mode, or being a tourist, or an adventurer, but we have permission to take on life afresh.

So have now work for you. Allow this moment to paint your life the way you want to, on your own canvas. If you wait for life to be perfect, you may remain stagnant. Imagine what it could be like, wherever you go, and the power of making the decision may flow over into other areas of your life.

Write down a few reasons that allow you to do it now: Why now?

If I did it now, it would solve this problem

If I did it now, I could do the following:

See tips and actions tips on:
www.FromOfficeChairToDeckChair.com

Chapter 2
You Don't Have to Quit Your Job

If you are not self-employed you may get panic attacks around money. "Ah, where is the money going to come from?"

Well, thanks to the internet and being a traveller, nowadays you may be in a great position. You may be able to continue your job from abroad, especially if you take calls, or do work on computers.

Have exploratory discussions about how you can work from home, and how that works. If you can work from home, can you also work from abroad?

The world is changing. At the start of my travels, I met people who could get work as bar staff, or teaching English, and the cost of being in another country was much cheaper, so they could live on savings. Students were able to take a year out, on a few savings made in temporary work.

Now, the world is different. Look to think globally and work locally. Developing a way to run a business online is much more accessible. Instead of internet cafes, so many more people have laptops, or smartphones, and the cost of internet access and wifi has plummeted.

Sometimes taking an idea from your own country can make you an expert in the place you live. You may spot an opportunity in the country you visit. I met people on the beach importing chickens, yes chickens, back to their own country.

As a traveller, you may be feted as an expert; it can work both ways. Speaking opportunities, or ways to learn.

Speaking English is always useful to communicate, with many different nationalities.

Keep your eyes open, you can also learn different cultural approaches, and learn both ways.

Certain professions are also useful, if you are a doctor , or accountant, some things can travel, others you may need to do exams. In the end, skype back to your country, or developing a business or entrepreneurial approach is what I saw working best on my travels.

What skills do you have that you could take abroad, and what could you learn abroad?

Skills:

_____

_____

What could I learn:

_____

_____

For ideas for setting up work, and working visa options:
www.FromOfficeChairToDeckChair.com

Working via Skype

So, what can you do via Skype? Anything that involves a call, or video. Teaching, conferences, teaching languages. Support calls to settle claims, or presenting online and doing teachings.

Maybe having a travel blog or sharing information about your destination.

I also met several people who re-invented themselves when they moved to another destination. Skype is one option, but also look at Facetime from Apple, and Google+, which have free calling systems. Whatsapp is offering calls , and many apps are coming online now.

Even music lessons can be given over Skype. A common approach is to do teaching either one-on-one or in groups via skype. If you need to take on bigger groups there are several providers who do conferences and calls. You may wish to take on one of these as they are evolving each year.

One feature of skype, that is not always used, is the sending of documents very quickly. Students can submit homework, but make sure your skype is turned off. Another alternative is google documents, which allow people to upload and share documents in common, and also work on several aspects of a project together. This is very good as access is via invitation and is password-protected.

In 2004, Skype was a relatively new phenomenon, but now it is becoming more common. It is easy to install, and is a free service via wifi. Make sure you have decent headphones or a microphone if your laptop is not of good quality.

If you need to, you can also look at businesses internationally, and check the time-zone differences, for your Skype calls.

As part of a club, I have a concierge service that I use for wake-up calls, and I can keep in touch with people quite easily with skype and Viber. Some people use WhatsApp, but that is more for messages.

To have a group conference call was a paid service on skype; on Google+ it is free, but there are less users as of this date. Google can add people just via their email.

Vonage is a useful service to have on travels, and operates via a base station, connecting to the internet. You can have a local landline number come to a phone connected to the computer. So you can still use the computer, or be on a phone while someone else is on the computer.

Have a credit card that can either top up skype automatically, or do that on request. Beware of accepting people you do not know, who can send documents that hack your account. Have a way to be in touch with people, should your account get hacked.

How can you prepare: what Apps are useful?
What cards do you have, or could have for travelling?

Apps:

_____

_____

Cards for travelling:

_____

_____

See favourite apps on
www.FromOfficeChairToDeckChair.com

Teaching, Communicating Internet

Teaching can be done in schools, in cafes in person, or via the internet. Check out local access to get a decent speed. Just having an internet cafe may not be enough, if the time zones that you require fall outside of opening times. Not all countries have decent internet connections, and it is worth asking what is available at the apartment or place you will stay.

Some places require you to bring your passport to get a mobile phone, and to register with that, or with a local CPF – like an ID number card for Brazil. So matters like phones, internet and mobiles may need a bit more to get started when you arrive. Be sure to check that your mobile is supported, and check the type of microchip as well. Do check with your service provider that your phone is unlocked so that you can use a local SIM card, which will save you a small fortune on access to calls and wifi, should your internet at home encounter problems.

Learn how to use your phone to access the internet, and be able to go via wifi on your laptop to connect to your phone's wifi. In this way, your phone becomes a sort of base station. Simple, just check this via google for your latop/phone, or ask a kid under 11 years old.

Teaching can be a great tool for connecting with the local people; making contact with them and giving back. Some people just do the teaching themselves, others take on organising groups. The choice is yours.

If you can operate online, you may keep international rates, and live at local prices. Not a bad idea, but check how you can receive payments, paypal, credit cards etc.

Again, if you are going to a remote area, you may not have good internet connection, so teaching may be more local, or a way of bartering for accommodation and food.

I was offered to stay at a hostel for free, in return for demonstrating an almost instantaneous skin care system that I had shown the hostel owner. However, I did have a commitment to return to my friends in another city the next day.

Meetup.com and some international groups exist to connect people who travel, or are new to cities. Each group has a different flavour.

What can I learn/teach whilst abroad?

_____

_____

_____

_____

Get a Sabbatical

Clearing the time sends a message to those around you, that you are moving abroad for a time. I did meet people on travels who were on sabbatical. Sometimes with a placement, sometimes just time off.

This allowed them to try being abroad, but also have a space to return back to work when they returned to their home country. This is important, so do see if this works as an option.

In one case, there was a couple from France, who had the option to try out living abroad, and then if it did not work out, their employer had their job waiting for them, in either 1 or 3 years.

Amazing. You may wish to see if that would be possible in your work.

Some people would also take up studies, or go into collecting, or studying abroad, with the acquisition of knowledge abroad being of benefit for when they returned home. That is up to you.

We sometimes can clear a year, in a sabbatical, which makes us think and act, and return to our profession with a new perspective.

Do you need to speak to someone to clear a possible sabbatical, or hold some post or work open for you? How could you do that? Would it be good for them to have you as a contact abroad?

I need to speak to:

_____

_____

_____

_____

My favourite sabbatical joke:
A couple, desperate to conceive a child, went to their priest and asked him for advice. "I'm going on sabbatical to Rome," he replied, "and while in Rome, I'll light a candle for you to conceive a child."
When the priest returned 3 years later, he went to the couple's home and found the wife pregnant, busily attending to two sets of twins. Delighted, the priest asked her where her husband was so that he could congratulate them together.
"He's gone to Rome, to blow that candle out!!" she replied...

www.FromOfficeChairToDeckChair.com

19

Identify Yourself as an International Person in the New Country

The perspective of being international can often be an advantage. Back home, we are just another Brit, Scot or American, depending where we live. When I arrived abroad, suddenly I was exotic. The Englishman. The person who was different. With that comes a few assumptions:

- Will be on time
- Will be polite
- Will be honest
- Likes to drink tea
- Speaks British English as distinct to American English

Other matters that you wish to bring can make you of interest. You have travelled, you can tell them about your own country. Britain has a reputation, and it is worth brushing up on a few parts of history. In Rio, music from the UK is loved, especially the Beatles, Rolling Stones and artists from the 1960s and 1970s. Amazing. People could not speak English, but they could sing whole verses and songs from the Beatles, in tune, and with a lovely Brazilian accent ...

Being international also helps with connecting into the ex-pat or international community. Being open to the local culture, and listening for what is loved about your own country. However, you are of your country, but not necessarily an ambassador. Sometimes you may have to break through stereotypes of your own culture, and that is part of the fun! People were often shocked that I could dance, and in time! Also that I did not need to get drunk...

Being an osteopath was also a rarity, so sometimes your profession may not be well known when you travel. Being open to the local approaches was refreshing.

Some friends would also take on a different persona, when travelling, and try their hand at selling art, or working on a boat. Things they had never ventured into when back home in the UK.

Remember, you are also an English speaker. There will be many people wishing to speak and practice their English with you. You may also have different ways of approaching work and your profession. Look to how things are done locally, and notice what you can bring to your travels. You may wish to choose a slightly smaller town, as capitals abound in English teachers.

Being international is a great gift, and some aspects, like work, breaks, communicating and friendships, take some patience and fun.

There is an ex-pat community, but this was quite distinct to the local community. For me, being international was great, and allowed me to notice what was me, and what was of my country. A great place to explore.

What can you bring to the table, as an international traveller? Customs, language, experience, stories, etc

_____

_____

_____

_____

www.FromOfficeChairToDeckChair.com

Consulting, Investments

Your international experience may allow you to consult, to advise on how matters are done in your home country. Your experience of work, and asking and agreeing to do things can be of value, as can advising locals how to deal with people in your own country. In Brazil, they love to ask about family, and personal matters. They are not too concerned with punctuality.

Explaining how matters are dealt with back in the UK helps to allow communication to flourish. What is needed for friendships, what is needed for trust. Advising what to expect next. A way to deal with work, what is expected when travellers visit a particular country. There are many ways that we can be of service to other travellers, and to hotels, businesses and people receiving other people from back home.

There may be opportunities to learn about investments. Here is an area in which to tread carefully. Laws may be quite different, even to the extent of seeing a lawyer, I was regularly advised to be careful, even if someone was a professional. Get to know several people and find people who are recommended and known to people you trust.

In Brazil, you need a CPF if you have to make an investment. Be sure to evaluate documents, investments and agreements carefully. You may see opportunities, but taking advantage really depends on what is involved, how well you know the people, and what is the upside and downside.

I saw opportunity in Brazil, in Rio, from about 2006/7. I was at the beach, and 2 things began to happen. First, they were developing the metro, and looking to the areas , the favelas around the metro line, it became evident that these had to be safe. Then, the conversation on the beach began to change. From conversations about women, clubs, music, parties, the conversations also began to cover oil contracts, deals, and visits by European companies, or insurance companies sending their staff to Rio, for the New Year. This was in contrast to previous years, where the conversations were not like that.

However, taking advantage of what that meant was a different matter. So you have to see, or start asking the question: What can I do? With whom can I partner? Can I do this alone, or do I need someone else?

Some people see opportunity, but start talking about stock markets... well, you decide, but I prefer to be a little bit more in control. Decide what works for you and your personality.

Be open to investments; it may be taking something from your country to the country you are visiting, or vice versa. You may be surprised, but it takes looking with that question in mind. Enjoy.

What is valuable

What are the regulations for investing?

How much capital is required, are there any laws on taking money in/out of the country?

_____

_____

_____

_____

An Opportunity to Change

It just might be that moving to another country allows you to change entirely. I met people who took on being a tourist guide, or teaching English, or even dancing; things they had NEVER done back home.

Others took on teaching cooking, or being a chef. You may be surprised when you arrive, that you love to do something new, or you get inspired to branch into something new. I met people even taking on opening up pousadas, or hostels for travellers. They did not need a big life, just a place to stay and take on receiving other travellers. Or they would settle with locals, and support them in their business.

Again, being a foreigner in a foreign country, you suddenly become a bit different, if only because you can speak English, or your mother tongue, to any travellers visiting the same country. With the advantage that you can have more trust through the language you can marry the two, and show people around.

I found that I had a love for the local music, and ended up dancing with the Brazilians at the London 2012 paralympic games closing ceremony. Certainly something not on the cards before I went to Brazil.

What other changes did I see? People taking on consulting, teaching, or learning about the local cuisine. Importing items from their home country.

What would you love to try? Sometimes travel opens up new ideas and we see things that we would love to do.

Or we get a different perspective on life, and trade up or down, or find that other things begin to matter. Sometimes we join a community, or even take on volunteer work. So much more becomes available.

I met people who would take on travelling, and just fund their way around the world, by renting out their home.

Sometimes travel just does that.
I met people doing a thesis, or doing an online business, but being in a warm climate. This is really for you to try, and you never know what you may run across on your travels.
Be inspired.

If you could wave a magic wand, and everything is alright, what would you like to be doing now?

Jot down some ideas:

_____

_____

_____

_____

www.FromOfficeChairToDeckChair.com

Chapter 3
Learn What Needs to be Done

Compare Living Expenses

When I went to Brazil the first time, it was amazing how cheap it was, for almost everything. Rentals, hotels, food, travel. The pound was so strong compared to the local economy. It was so cheap, a couple I met recounted the following: "After taking into account the plane fare, tours and accommodation, it was cheaper to go to Brazil for 8 weeks than to stay in London."

Now, times have changed, so the pound has weakened, since 12 years ago, and accommodation is no longer as cheap as it used to be. But relatively speaking, beer and eating out is still far cheaper than in the UK.

Some clothing is now cheap, but other items such as books in English are relatively expensive. Also there is a premium on imported goods, so an English Breakfast tea is 3-4 times the amount in the shops, and the same for Swiss chocolate.

So check that out where you go – and think in 2 ways: how much it is to live, compared to your money in the bank, and then compared to what money you can generate whilst travelling. What is available for you to do, that can allow you to pay for things locally?

There are other matters to take into account: With some rentals you may be responsible for repairs, or the air conditioning unit, or extra local taxes. Be clear on this before you sign, or get local advice.

You may keep down expenses by having shared accommodation, or living with a host family, who can guide you on shopping etc.

What about transportation? Is it worth getting a car, or hiring a car? Are your papers in order, to rent a car? In Rio, for example, you may have to think about parking spaces, and leaving cars on the street. Or do you have secure parking?

Locally, the way of life may bring up different expenses. In Europe, we have good access to airlines in between countries. In Brazil, there are offers, but you have to ask locally or have a service that tells you about similar services for cheaper travel. Another option is taking an overnight bus or coach. The distances are often just right, and it can save money. Be aware of getting to and from the coach station safely by taxi, yet again a consideration beyond the norm in Europe.

What do you need on a day-to-day basis? Car, phone, internet, shopping, clothes

_____

_____

_____

_____

How much does internet cost? What about mobile phone costs, and your cost to roam? The better option is to get a local SIM card. Can you get internet included in your accommodation? Which local cards give you access to mobile internet, and how much is the daily allowance? Will you need a change of wardrobe for the new climate? European clothes, even t shirts, are normally too heavy for a tropical climate.

www.FromOfficeChairToDeckChair.com

Look at Letting Out Your Property

If you own your property in the UK or home country, there are now several services you can use to generate income. This is not for everyone. Some people do not want strangers in their home, but may be comfortable with a friend, or friend of a friend staying at their home.

This is good for insurance purposes, so you are still covered in the event of an accident, or damage. Check your own insurance policy.

There are also short-term lets, or services like Airbnb. Check if you can do this, and have someone like a neighbour or trusted friend or family check them in/out. If you own that is fine; if you rent, you will have to check that your rental agreement allows you to sub-let.

You may wish to secure your possessions in a separate room, or set them aside, so that communal items are not anything of particular value. Be clear with people staying in your home, what they are to cover, if they pay anything, and what to do in an emergency. Gas contracts for boiler failure and central heating are also worth having, so that in an emergency the gas company is already paid. Some people use temporary storage, which is a financial choice to consider.

I met someone in Rio, who does a house swap service, and stays in amazing homes all over the world, in return for people staying in her flat in Copacabana. This is a very good idea, but you have to be sure that those people staying in your home have a place where you want to travel, and vice versa. There is no exchange of monies, which may suit your situation better, and also a certain comfort that you both respect each other's home.

This may generate enough to cover your living and travel expenses, to a point. Also, be clear what will happen when you return from travels, and if you were to have to return early. Most of this can be addressed up-front. Airbnb is useful as the time is normally just a few days, instead of a few months.

You may take the view that having someone you know and trust is as important as the money generated, so a good figure for staying can be agreed. However, on return, I know of people who offered a good mate's rate, only to have the people stay on, "because I can't find anything". So offering a decent rate can prevent people from moving on, when you may wish your home back!

All in all, if you own your own home, it can be an asset to generate income, but make sure you have agreements in place.

Preparing to move:
Letting agencies, sub-letting, or selling:
Your options are:

_____
_____
_____
_____

www.FromOfficeChairToDeckChair.com

Documentation, Visas and Financial Considerations

Although the UK has easy access to other countries, the terms of your visa may only allow a few months. There are times when it may be extended, so do check. If you have employment, or are on business or investing, you may get a working visa, all of which is worth preparing well in advance. In Brazil, there are short term, intra company visas; temporary work visas are valid for up to 2 years, but do not allow you to change profession. A permanent visa for investors requires a minimum amount of investment. Check with the embassy for your country for up-to-date information. Some cases like marriage or children allow people to qualify.

In some countries, it is also advised to have shots. Yellow fever shots were recommended for me, and these last for some 10 years. You can check online to find the updated medical advice, or check with your doctor, or local health service.
In Brazil it is easier to operate with something called a CPF. This allows rentals, investments, and even internet contracts or buying a mobile phone to be done much more easily. Well worth the initial bureaucracy of standing in queues and at banks.

Opening up a bank account is helpful, but money transfers are quite easy today. Do check. Brazil is quite restrictive in opening an account unless you have a working visa, or investment requirements.

There is also a tax on taking money or transferring money into Brazil, which was introduced a few years ago. So be aware of any currency restrictions into and out of the country.

Having a credit card is great, and even having 2 is advisable. If one goes missing, you have a backup. In some bars, they will accept Visa but not Mastercard, or vice versa. American Express is not common in Brazil, or many countries outside of the USA.

If you do carry a debit card, beware of replacing it; will your bank send it only to your UK address? What insurance is in place? Being without a debit card when travelling is not fun.

Credit cards tend to become expensive. There are also temporary cards that you can top up, that are more like debit cards, but you are limited to what can be lost if your cards or wallet are stolen.

Be sure to tell your credit card company and bank that you are travelling, and know what the procedures are for reporting, ahead of this happening. They may put a block on your card, even if still on you, if you have not told them you are travelling. This is just to protect you.

Having your internet banking set up is great. It may also be a good idea to carry some cash and have it in 2 places, for the same reason, in case of an emergency. It is also common practice to carry ID in some countries, which we are not used to in the UK. So having a card version of your driving licence is good. A paper copy of your passport is great, instead of wandering around with your actual passport.

What do you need to set up to prepare, from the above?

Documents
visas, ID, credit card, insurance

Back-up in Case of Emergency

Knowing your credit card and debit card numbers is essential, or having them all noted in one place, so one phone call can sort things out if they are lost. I have a service or two that covers this.

Keep a paper copy, or have something saved but encrypted in a way that only you can tell the real information. Keep sensible. Have something on the cloud, but encrypted.

Make sure you have backup funds, or someone you can speak to, to carry over until replacement cards arrive. Some banks even have a way for you to take out money when a card is lost. Do check if this applies when you go travelling.

It is also useful to have a backup or a way to block your phone in case of an emergency. There are many apps, or in built security on smart phones these days, so that a stolen phone gets locked or blocked and is relatively useless to a thief. Get the IMEI number noted, and send yourself an email with it. This may be required for insurance and a police report, so being prepared saves you loads of time, and gives a bit more peace of mind.

The apps may also send out an alarm via your phone, which will make the thief less likely to keep it on them, if it is screaming out "Stop me, I've been stolen!!"

Having copies of travel documentation and any ID is useful again, if something were to ever happen. Having these on the internet means that it can save time in an emergency. Does your travel cover you in such eventualities?

I also find that backup energy supplies for the phone are useful. A solar charger, or a portable charger which will do 1, 5 or 10 re-charging of your phone , is great when out and about.

Having a spare mobile is very useful, as is a backup SIM card for another operator, in case one mobile operator has poor service in that area. The spare mobile is just in case. Also a smart phone and laptop or tablet, in case one device gets damaged. Back up information that is not specific to one device but can be accessed from a computer. Beware of backing up financial information, which can be valuable if it falls into the wrong hands.

What are your backup plans?

_____

_____

_____

_____

Learn Enough of Local Culture, Medical Systems, Transport and so on

Learning about the local culture is tailored to how you will be living. It may all start from the airport. In Rio de Janeiro, if you are elderly or have small children, you are invited to a faster queue at the airport, at passport control. Very nice.

Transport covers taxis and buses, and previously, vans. Taxis are set apart, those that are official, and those that seem to be official. For the trip from the airport, you may pay 20-30% more to have a pre-paid taxi. Until you get to know the local culture, that may be worth it. Having a local person, or a person who knows the lay of the land, is a good idea, in another continent.

I remember arriving in Sao Paulo, and being told to visit someone's cousin. It gave a point of reference, someone I could trust, someone I could visit, and someone I could call on, who was not with a vested interest to sell me a holiday, or make money out of me. It soon became apparent that this was not a place to walk around with fancy watches, a smart jacket or a laptop on display. Be aware of these matters. In some countries, jaywalking will earn you a fine. I also noticed many tables in Rio, set for 4 people, but with a couple sitting on the same side, and sharing the same view. This is normal. Learn the nuances, of what is polite and what is not polite. How people greet each other, with a kiss on the cheek, or how business is conducted. How people relate to time is quite a culture shock in Rio as I write, and is even more flexible in the north of Brazil.

Medical matters are good to have covered by insurance before you travel. There are often good dentists in other countries, and a different level of coverage. You may have some coverage, but be aware not to automatically go to the hospital recommended by a concierge. I found I did have travel insurance, but the paperwork to go through, just to recover £50-150 on insurance, was prohibitive. Check, but notice that public health services abroad may not match the NHS in the UK.

On transport, how do people behave in traffic? What are the nuances of local travel? In Rio, until recently, cars would habitually go through red lights after 10 pm, and it was a surprise to find out why. Buses may be okay, but again may not be the same safety as we are used to in UK and Europe. Most of the time it was okay, and then I took vans which could be quick and convenient, but these were not controlled by the bus companies, and certainly there were times when I did not want to get inside a van, and let it go on. Be sure to follow your instinct. My friends in Rio would often read the crowd ahead of us, and sometimes cross the road, to avoid a small group of youths, even as young as 9 years old. It is a different world.

Also, be aware when people come up to you, of what is normal to ask. In Rio, there are clocks and temperature signs all over the streets, so it is not usual for someone to ask for the time. The best response is just to guess it, not to take out your phone or turn your fancy watch to display.

Notes, as you travel, on culture etc

_____

_____

_____

_____

www.FromOfficeChairToDeckChair.com

Build a Network of Acquaintances or People Who Can Help

I found I made a load of contacts, made up from people I was recommended to visit, and those I met on my travels. Having some volunteer project, an interest to bring you together, or work is a good start. People look to you differently if you are active, as opposed to just being a tourist.

Knowing people from different sources also helps to keep a perspective. Some friends are very traditional, and safe, and some are more adventurous. It helps to have different perspectives. Establishing trust takes time, and other countries may have a different level of what is normal and accepted.

In some countries, that network can be useful in several ways:

- What is going on today?
- Where shall I do my shopping?
- Who can help me find a place to live?
- Who wants to learn English?
- Participating in the local community, and staying safe.

Most events are great, just keep a perspective; having a network opens up many ideas. If I were to depend on just one or two people, I would get a very limited view of how it was to be in each city.

There is no place called Rio de Janeiro, I would say that there is the experience that we create with other people in Rio de Janeiro. So each traveller or person coming through will create it in their own way. When in Rome, …

I found that having local people was a resource when a bicycle got stolen, or when I lost my keys to the flat. People to step in, or also people to plug in and let me know about parties on the beach, or shop openings. Sometimes taking on new experiences that I might not do on my own, like samba around a table, by the beach in Rio, at night, free of charge, just buy your own drinks... priceless.

Local people can set you straight on connecting your phone and also dealing with any problems in the local language. It is amazing how well my Portuguese was for ordering items, but if there was a problem with mobile phones, then suddenly I had developed a thick accent. So a local can set things straight.

Also, local people get better prices, and know the best way to get from A to B so taxi drivers do not try it on so easily. Having local support helps when walking out and about, and also makes going to the beach easier, because you have people to look after your valuables.

It is also a way to get invited to special events and parties, and to be of service to several people there. I did get called to visit people who were quite ill, to see what I could do to help. Again, priceless.

List of people you know at the destination:

_____

_____

_____

_____

www.FromOfficeChairToDeckChair.com

Chapter 4
Set up Lines of Communication

Keep Your Clients Informed, or Your Work Too

"Wise men talk because they have something to say;
fools, because they have to say something."
- Plato

Let clients know that you will be abroad. In some cases you will still be able to deal with clients via skype or email. It all depends on your profession. Do check the time difference, and how that changes over the seasons. A time difference may change dramatically if you are moving from Northern to Southern Hemisphere across the seasons.

Allowing others to deal with your clients in your absence may be another way to deal with their needs. The more notice that clients have, the better. You may wish to have a separate skype account for business clients only.

You can also use a service that diverts your calls, or allows you to take calls via a landline to your computer, via a VOIP service. Skype, Vonage and various others fit the bill here too. Contact me to get a refer-a-friend offer from Vonage.

There are also conference call numbers, which allow you to ring in from a local landline, say in Rio, and speak to a group of people who ring in from all over the world with a PIN number. We use this in a group, which covers 28 countries as I write. Very useful, and a way to access calls via a local call.

If you are in health/medical profession, you may need to consider a locum or someone to cover your patients, and clients whilst you are away.

Lines of communication may then be to the locum, or the person standing in for you. It is great how much work can be achieved in just a few emails in a month. Keeping in touch via email, having a message system, can all keep your workload manageable, and allow you to continue working from abroad. Think about lines via text messages, but roaming charges are high for this, so have an automatic reply on your mobile system.

www.FromOfficeChairToDeckChair.com

Skype, Viber, Whatsapp

"When I wrote 'The World Is Flat,' I said the world is flat. Yeah, we're all connected. Facebook didn't exist; Twitter was a sound; the cloud was in the sky; 4G was a parking place; LinkedIn was a prison; applications were what you sent to college; and Skype, for most people, was a typo."
- Thomas Friedman

As written before, Skype, Viber and whatsapp are very popular ways to keep in touch. It would seem like emails are being used less, and messenger systems are developing. Services like Google+ also allow access to multiple messages, or sending messages to specific groups. As smart phones evolve, more of these apps will be working in future. And with 5G on the horizon, the speed of many apps is increasing.

Do check what information the app wants from you. Viber and facebook messenger became the way to communicate when I went to Rio. It seems to be replacing text messages, which are not included as unlimited on calling plans that I saw.

You can also message back to the UK, via wifi and data use, for an included price, which is much cheaper than sending a text message directly.

Viber has been useful, and gets tied to your phone, even if you put in another SIM card, the phone will still be recognised as you, by people who have your UK number.

The pace of change is so quick, it is good to just ask the locals, the younger people in 20s, or even teenagers.

So, together with these, go the data packages for internet that you can access via your phone

The app world is forever changing, so what apps do you know now, and ask around for apps that you may like to use when abroad. easier to prepare before you travel:

e.g. google maps, calculator, translating apps, and so on

_____

_____

_____

_____

_____

_____

www.FromOfficeChairToDeckChair.com

Look at Time Zones and How They Change Over Seasons

As mentioned before, working internationally does depend where you are moving to. Notice which countries you need to call in real time. For example, London to Rio has a 4 hour time difference in June, but a 2 hour time difference in December. So it is very easy to keep in touch and have overlapping hours during the months around December.

Time zones can also change within a country, and have changes from north to south. Places like Russia go through some 7 time zones, if I remember correctly. So where you are in the country is important.

Where Pays Better?

*"Anyone who lives within their means
suffers from a lack of imagination."*
- Oscar Wilde

Now, not being one to go against the great Oscar Wilde, but it does open up something when we go abroad.

So, you live in one country but have links back to another. How can you benefit from that? Living in Rio or Brazil, people can still provide telephone work or services back into London, and earn several times more than they might in Brazil. This may be covered by UK laws, so do check.

I fail to understand why people go to a foreign country, and then keep work going to earn money in their home country where they earn less than where they are staying. If you get what I mean...

Some people provide work, or consultancy from the country with cheaper workers, into the country which pays more for the same services. It is one possible strategy, but works if you have your own people working in both countries.

You may find anomalies. In Rio de Janeiro, computer programmers and tech support people seem to provide the most basic services. People will call out someone to set up their computer, or to install a webcam. Services that we now just google and get the information in English.

The pay is higher in:

_____

_____

_____

_____

Fill in the following:
The time zone difference is: ___ hours in the winter
and ___ hours in the summer

Set up Online Payments, Banking and Credit Cards

Set up to have your payments working online. You can pay your bills, check status, and pay off your credit cards. Having this done automatically is useful, but also a way to check your bill online is ESSENTIAL.

In London, we have auto payment as a very easy way to pay bills and credit cards, but it is even more important to have access from abroad. Surprisingly, there are still long queues in the banks in Brazil. One day they will catch up and allow bills to be paid, without visiting the bank.

Another benefit of travelling is that we see how far we have come in the UK, with how payments are made, and covered by certain guarantees.

I have set up the following automatic payments

_____
_____
_____
_____
_____
_____
_____
_____

www.FromOfficeChairToDeckChair.com

Do you need to speak to your bank? Credit card company? Do you know the contact numbers before you travel?

Mobile Phones and Vonage

> *"It's easier for a rich man to ride that camel through the eye of a needle directly into the Kingdom of Heaven, than for some of us to give up our cell phone."*
> - Vera Nazarian

As stated before, do get a local SIM card on your mobile. Check if you can unlock your mobile before you go travelling. It is possible to have this done for about US$10 online, but that may take some time. SIM cards now come in different sizes, from old fashioned, to the newer smart phones mini SIM cards. You may need to have the local mobile provider help you insert the new type of SIM card. Some mobiles are not supported in other countries, The technical aspect is beyond me, but worth checking before you arrive, or when you get your next mobile phone.

Vonage is a godsend, in that local calls can come to your home abroad. People could call me on my London number, and it would arrive in my flat in Rio. All you need is a wifi base station.

Contact me on the link, to get an offer on Vonage and other operators.

www.FromOfficeChairToDeckChair.com

vonage request link

Chapter 5
Learn the Language

"England and America are two countries
separated by the same language."
- George Bernard Shaw

and

"To God I speak Spanish, to women Italian, to men French, and to
my horse - German."
- Emperor Charles V

Why, Oh Why?

Why learn the language? For me, it is why not? I just cannot sit in another country for long and not understand:

1   What they are saying to me
2   What they say to each other
3   Why they are laughing, and those jokes and songs ...

The why is what drives all learning. Grab a context for learning, that shifts what is possible as you live abroad.

How do you love to learn?

_____

_____

_____

_____

Give Yourself Time

"The two hardest tests on the spiritual road are the patience to wait for the right moment and the courage not to be disappointed with what we encounter."
- Paulo Coelho

Yes, it may take a few days, weeks or months, so allow yourself enough time to plan. As part of this, the start is important. Use that time responsibly. You may wish to speak every day, or take classes, or use other key strategies.

Key Strategies for Learning a Language

- say something every day
- practice key things from the day before
- have a good reason
- allow yourself to jump in and play with it
- immerse yourself with people who cannot speak your mother tongue

Find topics that you really do want to speak about – bring a favourite, but simple book. If it is interesting, you can be interested to share that with other people. Keeping it simple really works.

Keep It Simple

Get most of your words out. Copy phrases, and listen to when people speak and copy it immediately in the moment. Use the same phrase, and SPEAK it. It is no good just listening and nodding, unless you want to become a nodding dog …

Allow repetition to get you through the speaking. Do not worry too much about grammar in the beginning, just listen carefully and COPY.

Jump In and Open Your Mouth

This is a great start. There is no place to get to, or rehearse. As a newbie, you are always in the place to start. Give yourself permission to make mistakes. It really does not matter; if you want to communicate, that counts for so much more.

Open your mouth and start to speak, and listen to how it comes out. And play.

Some people look to their books, which is all well and good. But the people who speak very day soon get the hang of speaking. Trying to speak their language is a great way to make new friends.

Practice Groups and Resources

There are groups with foreigners, or others who are practicing the language. Best of all is with an international group, but where the foreign language is spoken by locals. Some people use tv, but I find that the speed is too much when first there.

Another useful resource is youtube – a video of your favourite programme, film or comedian, with subtitles. This is a more passive way to get the language, but it works.

Find a way to be creative:
• Practice in situations where you cannot use your mother tongue, the language you speak normally. That way, you HAVE to use the foreign language.

- Play games, be competitive, find something that has you wanting to learn.
- Most importantly, find something that you can choose to get good at, and which has you speaking.
- Create ways to say something each day. Learn to sing a song in your chosen language, so you can join in when people are singing.
- Take a song or a joke, that you know well in your own language and translate it – obviously a joke that translates well, and does not depend on puns, since these may be language-specific.

What phrases do you keep on hearing? What do people talk about in general? What would you like to learn to say? What would you like to understand? Have a great reason for learning a language, and the creativity follows.

www.FromOfficeChairToDeckChair.com

Chapter 6
Live, Don't Just Visit

"I can't think of anything that excites a greater sense of childlike wonder than to be in a country where you are ignorant of almost everything.
- Bill Bryson

Living in another country is a different mindset than just visiting. What do I mean by that? Well, consider how you are when you visit a place for a day or two. You may go out all the time, visit a few tourist places, and interact more with tourists, and famous attractions.

When you live in another country, you begin to adopt the way they do things. Try out the local food. Notice how they eat breakfast, and what they have for breakfast and other meals. For example, in Rio, it is common to have a coffee and a misto quente, (ham and cheese on toasted bread), or pao de queijo, small bread/pastry based on cheese, freshly squeezed juice, or a 'vitamina' like a fruit shake, or banana shake with protein powder.

Eating the local food and drinks helps to savour a country. Another aspect of life in Rio is coconut water – a refreshing clear sweet liquid straight from the coconut, best drank chilled. Another beverage is caldo de canaa, a sugar drink, from sugar cane, which is crushed through a special machine, to produce a green liquid. It is surprisingly refreshing and suitable to the tropical climate.

Also the way they drink beer in Rio is 1 or 2 degrees, very cold, and straight from the bottle; or a larger bottle shared between several people, and toasted in the middle of the table. Snacks are available, and served to share between the table. Ask the locals and get to see life from inside their customs.

Living also involves seeing how they shop; the way they use markets for fresh fruit and vegetables. The abundance of fish markets, and being able to take fish straight from the market, and have it cooked for you, in bars upstairs or alongside the market is a wonderful feature too.

In Rio, and Brazil, I was often told of shopping centres and shopping malls. I could not understand why these were the source of such pride. Then, after wandering up and down the streets in 30-40 degrees C, I understood. The shopping malls are air-conditioned. They have security, so less beggars and problems. They are great in the day for a snack, some shopping, and escaping the boiling sun at lunchtime.
Then at night, the food halls all open onto one common area.
In some cities, there is live music and dancing, - Forro - in these shopping areas, so a great place to have a drink and a dance.

Let the locals take you to some events, such as live roda de samba - musicians around a table, singing, where everyone joins in the singing and dancing. A fair of local goods. A visit to waterfalls, and a walk or trek. Festivals particular to times of year.

In Brazil, a local will take you to places, and also you may find a difference in price as you become part of the community. This also means participating, and helping out with people there. The experience is quite different to just staying with the ex-pats, but again, it depends on who you meet, and your own attitude and luck.

Go Beyond the Vacation

Extending your stay beyond a vacation means different things in different locations. You may visit an area, like I did in Itacare, which is a small holiday destination. Charming and lovely, and great for 1-2 weeks. As a city person, I would have had to adjust my thinking to stay longer, as I had began to repeat going to the same cafes and bars in just that short time. Then it depends on what you like for stimulation, or if you are happy being in a more quiet area.

Staying beyond a vacation, to me, requires participating at some level past the 1-2 weeks of being new. The larger the city, the easier to find a mix of places to visit. What activities can you do?

Beyond the vacation, you begin to point towards setting down roots or activities to, again, interacting with the local community.

What does that mean?

It might be launching an idea into that city or country. It may be reporting, or having a blog about your experiences in that city. I have met journalists who have become the local reporter for news channels back in their home cities.

What would you be happy to do, once the novelty of the place has worn off? Taking on a project or giving talks, or learning something structured is always great. Allow other travellers to be a source.

A stay in the sun can be great, but normally something kicks in and we wish to give back, or be empowered and empowering in our new location. Being prepared for this can save time, and keep the experience fresh.

Travelling or moving with someone also allows you to inspire each other, or do some projects together.

www.FromOfficeChairToDeckChair.com

What Is Local?

"When in Rome, do as the Romans do."

What is local, and what is international? I have used this question to help me decide some experiences. I can go into, say, a Starbucks and have a coffee, but then I could be ANYWHERE in the world. Going into a stylish local coffee shop, or a simple coffee shop with history, may be a change.

Local can also mean getting to know local customs, and areas that the locals frequent. Local can be the food places they use, or the bars where the locals sing. I did meet some Americans, on an international MBA programme, where they had opted for time in Rio. It sounded like a dream placement. We chatted, and shared about music, and they had just gone to American/European flavoured bars and music venues; places they could have experienced back home. There is nothing wrong with that; we do all need to come back into our own culture. I showed them some videos of the music places I was going to, and they could not believe the difference!

Local may be, also, seeing how they do Sunday lunch, or being invited in with families to anything, such as a BBQ. In Minas Gerais, I remember being invited to a BBQ. One of the city's top lawyers was there, together with a gardener from next door, and a lady who cleaned houses. This mixing of people was quite refreshing, and again, something of which I do not see too much back in London.

Local may also mean being tolerant. Noticing that they may play music out of the back of cars, at petrol stations. Neighbours may be used to playing music and having parties. Be aware and clued in to what is normal wherever you choose to live.

Some friends also showed me places to take a shower under a waterfall, to see views and go on walks in forests, off the beaten track. Going local also means going with people when they take a trip. I have been several times with Brazilians, where we were 15 -30 people sharing a flat or accommodation. That meant taking my own pillows and being prepared with mosquito repellant.

www.FromOfficeChairToDeckChair.com

Experiences

> *"Nothing ever becomes real 'til it is experienced."*
> - John Keats

Be a collector of experiences. And allow yourself to know what you wish to experience. Some people went to Iguacu falls, and still rave about the experiences, as if it were a spiritual breakthrough!

I like to visit places that surprise: The fort at Copacabana beach has a great view to the beach going back, and cafes and live music playing there. On top of Santa Teresa, there are coffee shops, and some cool clubs.

My friends took me along waterfalls, and swimming and diving across a few of these in a day was a lovely experience.

New year in Rio de Janeiro, on Copacabana beach, 25 degrees on the beach, and over a million people were there. Fireworks , a beer in one hand, and singing to any one of several bands playing on one of the 6 stages; priceless.

Other experiences yet to come, but recommended, are to visit some of the spiritual guides or healers. I did go into the Amazon, and spoke via an interpreter to the local tribespeople, to discover some of their myths and legends.

An experience for me was even to visit in the countryside, and spend an afternoon in a hammock. It was great to try out things that were specific to that country, which I could not do elsewhere.

Volunteering is another great access to experiences. Finding something registered, before you head out, can save you time. There are many projects, and I even work with a company that does volunteerism as part of its remit.

**Find out more on
www.FromOfficeChairToDeckChair.com**

What Is Important to You?

"There is no passion to be found playing small – in settling for a life that is less than the one you are capable of living."
- Nelson Mandela

Establish what YOU wish to achieve. Once I arrived abroad, it was interesting to be able to make decisions with little or no reference to what I did back home. Do I want to meet these people? How do I wish to spend my day?

You may be like some people who find a lease of life to travel more; or others I met who went to local schools and volunteered in teaching. You may find that you love to teach English and meet the locals willing to learn. You may wish to immerse yourself in the local culture, or bring some of your own background to the locals.

Sometimes people take a hand in doing something completely different. Selling antiques, cooking, learning to dance, taking part in festivals, setting up their own NGO – all of these and more I encountered on my travels.

It may be that you wish to go into a local countryside, and lead a more simple life. Sometimes being abroad allows us to re-invent ourselves. We already stand out, as being the foreigner, and that attracts attention. People may listen to you a bit more, simply because you have bothered to travel to their country. You can also be a source of how to deal with people from your own culture and country.

Take a moment. Write down what is important to you, a whole list. Then, write another list of what you give your time to, on a weekly basis. There may be things that are important, but that do not feature very much in your activities...

We sometimes live a life that is a continuation of decisions made at a much younger age, to fulfil the wishes of a teenager. Travel allows us to review. I found, in my first visit to Brazil, that only once in three months was somebody rude to me. It was marvellous. I did not have to spend time with people whose company I did not like!

So what became important to me was the peace of mind. The connection, and freedom. Each traveller normally found something, merely by being abroad, for an extended time, beyond the 2 weeks of a normal holiday.

Allow yourself the space to review this every so often, be it every few months, or annually. It is a gift to yourself.

www.FromOfficeChairToDeckChair.com

Local Groups, Neighbours

Local groups help many things in your stay. Church and religious groups are always helpful, and a good way to get local knowledge and advice. Neighbours will know where to buy and source things. If you live in a block of flats, there will be a sindica, in Rio, who looks after security, payments, and will know most of the people living in the block.

The porters will be key in allowing you in. Make sure you get to know them by name. Be guided by the local people. Brazilians will ask personal questions from the start, but you are not required to give them chapter and verse in reply. Keeping a discreet distance about what you let on is a matter of common sense in another country.

Neighbours can help you find places to eat, shop, and orientate you to others coming in. Do be aware of living in a neighbourhood that matches who you are. If you are a quiet person, remember that parts of the world may think it normal to play ear-splittingly loud music at 8 am or 2 am …

Other parts may have wonderful quiet communities. It is good to find this out beforehand.

Once I took a room inside a recommended apartment, so I felt looked after by the owner, and not just a tourist taking a flat. However, I did have to draw boundaries about using my computer when I was not there. It may be okay if someone asks, but things can go missing at the touch of a button. Apple computers have a convenient guest feature for the laptop.

The locals often get better prices at markets. It is quite bizzare that the prices can go up, just because you are a foreigner, so just be aware. Locals will also know where to get furniture, and where is safe to visit. Do not rely on just one local person. It may take time to find a team of people who can advise on different aspects of local life.

In Rio, neighbours will ask you details, and will often know of your comings and goings. I discovered later that there are security cameras, that people can just check. The porters can also comment and know what you do.

Sometimes this network of people can provide magical connections, but remember you are in a foreign culture. The level of trust is easy on a basic friendship level, but be aware how foreigners occur locally.

Locals and Ex-Pats

Local people often jump at the opportunity to practice their English with you, or to learn about your culture. Find a few other areas which can be of interest. Local people can also be divided into friends, and those who 'work' with tourists, like guides. They may recommend you to their friend the taxi driver, and other people to visit or stay with. Again, take your time to befriend people. Latin Americans are very friendly, but sometimes you have to check how well you know people.

I have been invited to a concert at Urca, and Sugar Loaf mountain, after meeting some locals at the beach. At the end of a boat trip, the locals invited us to Lual, a beach party at night. I regret not staying, but I had made a commitment to a party in Ipanema.

Other times I found myself going to a huge concert way out of town, with people I did not know too well, and luckily found my way back.

At other times, it was a relief to find some ex-pats and revert to speaking English, with people who got the subtleties of English humour. Irish pubs were often a source for this. Other places also provided groups, meetups and online communities for ex-pats.

These allowed for beach parties, places to have a beer, or go on a tour aided by locals, or an ex-pat. This is a very useful resource, to connect with others who have been living there longer, to share and find out what works.

A useful place for talking business, with others who have done rentals locally, providing security, making websites, and throwing wine tastings. Also had access to some chic clubs, in the company of 100-200 people, helps to get things started quickly.

Ex-pats will often guide you as to where to go safely, and provide a place to connect with home. Not a bad idea; however much I loved being in Brazil, I did miss certain aspects of life in Europe, if only at the beginning, when it was great to speak, without stumbling over my Portuguese.

It also provided a place to speak to other people; Scandinavians, Americans and non-Brazilian people, just to get an international perspective again, and plug into another way to think and converse.

www.FromOfficeChairToDeckChair.com

Chapter 7
You Can Do This

"If you can dream it, you can do it."
- Walt Disney

Whether you think you can do this, or you think you cannot, you are right. Most of this is so do-able. It can take a balance of preparation, and action. Some things in life need preparation, and at times we just need to act, once we have sufficient information to make a decision.

Work out what you need to know:

- Accommodation
- Earning whilst travelling
- Language barriers
- Enjoyment
- Funding the move
- Contacts in the place.
- Safety
- Health

Add what you need to this list. Look to tailor some of the trip or adventure, to what you need. Then take the action. A successful friend of mine said this once about a property deal, in relation to due diligence:

The mark of an entrepreneur is that they take all the facts about that deal, and then they make a decision. We can never guarantee what will happen in future, but we can take in enough information to make an informed decision and then act. An entrepreneur will gather as much information as possible, and then decide.

This works very well for travelling. I found that, at times, not knowing was another way to travel. It is great to be prepared, but then when things are cancelled, or change, life still goes on, and out of changes of plan maybe new days, new friends or new opportunities arise.

What has you do this is the sense of why. Then take that action – be it booking your ticket, or getting your shots, or renewing your passport. Each day something will bring you closer to your dream, and then you can make it come true. Some people may just like to arrive in a new country and wing it. But when we cross continents to another culture, the same rules of behaviour do not necessarily apply. So, preparation is key.

Look for what you can do in this. What is it that you NEED to know, and differentiate that from what you would LIKE to know. In the end, this is your adventure, your step into another life. What would that be like, what would be possible if you make this happen? What else could you make happen in your life? As they often say, it is not the things we do that we regret, but we often regret the things we did not do ….

www.FromOfficeChairToDeckChair.com

It May Be Easier Than You Think

So how hard is it to move to another country? There is some bureaucracy, some preparation, but here is the thing: When I asked a few people how much capital, or money, they would need to move to another country, I was quite surprised. $20,000 or $100,000 we the sort of sums quoted to me!!

Amazingly, I met lots of young people doing this, and it is possible to start with £2,000 a month budget – at least it was back in 2003. So have a float of some money, and a plan of how to earn, and make sure you allow for emergencies.

It cannot be that bad. There are refugees fleeing countries, and ending up elsewhere every few months. Many people have done this before you, so find out what works.

Chat to people on your holiday who have actually made that move. Surprisingly many do the move; not many do it going back and forth. The reason is, more often than not, love or marriage. That has people change country.

There are many imaginary obstacles to doing this. So, sit down with this book, and make a few notes of what you actually need. Add in some emergency money, add in health insurance, if you deem it necessary where you are going, and then act.

You may be able to negotiate time off work, if you are employed. Look to a sabbatical. Again a conversation may be all that is required. A conversation with your boss, your spouse, your relatives and friends, your colleagues.

A bit of perspective, from others who have done it:

Back in the 1980s, very few people travelled extensively. It would take maybe 5-6 weeks working as a waiter, to save up the money to travel into Europe, for the flight. A flight to Sweden from London was about £179 in 1979.

In 2014, a return flight to Sweden was about £150-190, but after inflation, that is well within working for a week or so. Cheap airlines can bring this down to about £100, including taxes etc...

So, the relative cost of travel, compared to basic salaries, is much cheaper in today's world.

Accommodation is more affordable, and we can stay very cheaply in hostels, and by booking accommodation online, whilst we look for long-term rentals.

And finally, the internet has brought down prices, and made it very cheap to keep in touch with our home countries, and run businesses from abroad. A true godsend.

Before it would have been only the super rich who could travel around the world and keep in touch. Now most people can have cellphones, and laptops and with that and the internet, do banking, business and leisure for a few pounds or dollars a month.

Do You Plan or Do You Jump In?

It's up to you. You can plan all you like, or you can jump in. Again, ask yourself the questions that you need the answers to. I got recommended one or two people to speak to, whilst in Sao Paulo, and a few people to meet. I had no grasp of the language, so that was very useful indeed.

Then I made the move to Rio, which was like a different country. Again I had some contacts there, and happened on people via others and introductions. After a few weeks, that had spread by change.

I did meet travellers, with rucksacks, or people leading a very sophisticated life. Some people like to jump in, not a care in the world, and just ride the day. DIt all depends on your take on life.

You may surprise yourself once you arrive.

A lovely combination is to do lots of planning, but be prepared to change plans, take risks and be spontaneous once you arrive and know the lay of the land. One point is that, if you are spontaneous, do have a person (s) informed of when to next meet you. So, be spontaneous, but send a message, saying you are going to a club, or island with so and so, and will be back on, say, Tuesday at 8 pm.

If going with relative strangers, let them know you have told others; that is just good practice.

Every so often a tourist will jump in, and be left shirtless. People tell me of meeting others in a club, or on the beach, and waking up with everything gone. Wallet, cellphone, passport, etc. Learn where to jump in and with whom.

But then some people do not take care, so be aware.

As another friend put it, in preparation, it is like ready, set, go ! Some people do: ready, ready, ready, ready, set, set set , … and others do: ready , GO!!

I have met many tourists who arrived in Rio, but were not aware of how to do things. They can be lucky, but they would waste a lot of time and money. My Brazilian friends would soon make sure that people were looked after, and accompanied to the right places.

For example, in Brazil, I never saw anyone hitch hiking, and very few people on cycle tours. That may be a reflection of the world today, but some of it is a local difference.

Choose Your Own Reasons

> *"It is our choices, Harry, that show what we truly are,*
> *far more than our abilities."*
> - J.K. Rowling

This is an area which is sometimes overlooked. We make decisions, and some of these may be conscious to please ourselves, or others; and some may be more unconscious. My reason was to take better holidays, and to have two summers a year. It was a deep-seated reason.

It was also to immerse myself in another country, into its culture. It was to see if I could make a life for myself. My Mum was from Scandinavia, and my Father's family goes back to refugees from Russia and Poland.

It was a mix of also leaving the UK over the short days of winter. A few things came together that allowed me to do that, and if I waited – well, maybe the chance would never come again.

Of course there were barriers: the language; the lack of contacts in a foreign country; not knowing where was safe; being a long way from home; travelling on my own. The reasons kept me going.

What I also discovered was a new sense of self-reliance, and resolve, when taken out of my normal environment, and placed into another. So, some of the reasons became apparent, once I had gone there. And these were benefits, which I may not have seen beforehand.

Also, my reasons for returning have changed each year. And it has been good to review my reasons. As time goes on, I have changed – some things have happened, or not happened as I have anticipated. I have reviewed if Brazil is just one of several destinations I could take on over the winter. Rather like having a favourite restaurant; it is good to try some other restaurants, and not only go to your favourite every time.

Also, places change. Some of the great music places in Copacabana have closed down – like Modern Sound, a CD and Bossa Nova establishment, which closed its doors. A few of my favourite restaurants have been replaced. The feel of the neighbourhoods has also changed, as have the tourists. Mostly this has been for the better, so the reasons for returning have changed too.

Allow yourself to be focused on the reasons, and review these as you go along. You may find yourself inspired, by a chance meeting. A chance acceptance of an invitation brings you into a new group of friends. Early on, I met someone who was handing out tourist leaflets for tours. I returned back to my flat to find her dropping a leaflet, and we struck up a friendship. A few years later, I was at her wedding to an Irish man, in Ireland. Funny how life can turn on a chance friendship.

www.FromOfficeChairToDeckChair.com

When It All Starts

"There are only two mistakes one can make along the road to truth;
not going all the way, and not starting."
- Buddha

There are a few theories as to when your adventure (or travel, or move) really starts. To some it starts when they land in the country; others when they have booked the plane ticket. This was something which had been simmering in the back of my mind for a while.

What I noticed was a series of coincidences, which clustered together, over a few weeks. Firstly I had broken up from my Brazilian girlfriend, and up to that point hardly knew Brazilians in London. Then I gave a presentation to a music school, London school of contemporary music, and there was a Brazilian musician. A few days later, I took a coffee in Oxford Street, and the barrista was Brazilian, and her boyfriend was that Brazilian musician!

Then, a few days later, a man sat next to me at a breakfast networking event, and he was from Sao Paolo. And in New York, I had met a group of Brazilians at an event in the middle of a Marriott hotel.

So, I decided to book the ticket – and everything began to fall into place. One of my patients had also been married to a Brazilian lady, so I was given some contacts to call in Sao Paolo and Rio. Another friend of my mum gave me his cousin to contact in Sao Paolo.

A month before going out to Brazil, I saw City of God, a great film, but quite shocking in its portrayal of life in the favelas of Rio. So I definitely had mixed feelings about visiting this country.

For sure, there was a time when I made the decision, and there was no going back. It fell into place, and certainly became more concrete with the purchase of a plane ticket. All other matters followed, like vaccinations, insurance, organising someone to stay whilst I was away. Letting people know I was away. The purchase of a laptop, which allowed travelling much easier, and being on the internet.

There is something that happens with the purchase of a ticket, or the booking of accommodation, which plants a stake in the ground at a certain date in the future. That makes everything work to that deadline. Oh, and by the way, in my case, there was no perfect preparation. I just did the best I could. In my circle of friends, I cannot recall anyone who had done this, in quite this way, at least to Brazil.

Some had gone to China, or Japan, or Singapore or USA. But this was mostly via work, or as an extended holiday. It gave an indication, and I could reference a few people who had done this, once I arrived in Brazil, but these were few and far between, and mostly people who had left their home country for good.

Nothing makes a decision seem more fixed than to commit to it by paying for a ticket or hotel, and to have a fixed date for that. Just saying – but notice when you take yourself seriously in this.

Allow It To Be a Mix – Imperfect and Spontaneous

> *"No matter how many plans you make or how much in control you are, life is always winging it."*
> - Carroll Bryant

As alluded to before, you may do all this preparation, but preparation is only that. We just have to deal with what happens, not only with what we PLANNED to happen. There is freedom and grace, and something fun, to go with the flow, and allow things just to be.

Occasionally, I did come across some travellers who would get caught up in comparing things that were not perfect, and allowed that to spoil their experience. Like some Americans, complaining that a beer was about US$2 in a hotel bar, (about £1.20) when they could get it for 40 cents in a local bar – but set in a much less smart environment. It was amusing to see people staying in a plush hotel (used by the Brazilian international football players) quibbling over US$2 for a beer...

Compare this to many locals, or people making do with fab food, and enjoying life, and joining in. Learning to roll with the punches, and remember this is a different culture.

If people were late, that was a space to take a drink, a beer, or a coffee and meet new people – a chance to use that time to browse, and learn, or change plans.

At one visit, where I was staying got broken into, and 2 cameras were stolen. So I left that flat, because someone appeared to have a copy of a key, since the door was not forced open. I only noticed the loss by going through my clothes. On the back of this, I was introduced to take a room in another area in Rio, much smarter, but with flat sharing.

We tried this for a week, on a trial basis, going both ways. It worked out fine for me. The added company was good, and the knowledge of staying with locals provided extra inclusion, and a sense of being orientated in a way that just renting a flat would not do. It was hard to put my finger on it, but it seemed that less would happen to me, as I was staying inside a local person's apartment.

If a visit was cancelled, or a place was full, being flexible allowed for other experiences to come about. Part of travelling was also to be with a change of plans; waiting around for people to get ready to get going; dealing with times when the electricity cut out, and having to walk down 11 flights, since the lift was out.

Once, a whole block suffered a power cut. It was 12.30 am and the air conditioner was out. Too hot to have the windows open, I changed plans, and took myself out to a local music place to have a beer, dance and listen to music. By the time I had returned a couple of hours later, the electricity soon came back on, but it sure was better than sitting in the dark, on a humid night!

At other times, I got caught in the rain, and found myself drenched through to the skin, as much as taking a swim in the sea. All there was to do was get to where I was going, dry off, and have a change of clothes. Take a coffee and add it to my diary. Fab.

Keep it Safe

As much as possible, be happy in your travels, but keeping it safe is generally a good motto. If not sure of an area, it may not be so good to wander around. Find out local knowledge.

Keeping it safe includes, but is not restricted to:

- take a taxi home if not sure
- safety in numbers, travel to places in pairs or more
- having a spare credit card
- keeping some money aside
- be aware at cashpoints and be discreet with money
- counting money inside shops and banks, and not on the street
- keeping by your bags, especially taking them with you when leaving a taxi

- use of your cellphone on buses, beware of kids snatching it through a window
- be aware of who is on the buses and the street around you
- avoid wearing gold, rings or necklaces which can be stolen easily
- have your cellphone password-protected
- dress down, and not conspicuously like a tourist
- inform others when you leave one place, when to expect you to arrive, or text them / call them when you arrive
- if something does happen, like a mugging, keep eyes down, be aware, and move as little as possible. Do not be a hero, as the rules are different here. Guns and knives may be carried. Is it worth it for a few dollars or cards?
- If people approach you who may be asking strange questions, be aware where more members of the public are. Approaching some large Brazilians, who look like security, to help to translate has made some unsavoury characters walk away
- having a small amount of cash in a top pocket or pocket to pay for buses or taxi fares, instead of taking out a wallet full of cash.
- Advising people if you are not coming home that evening.
- Going out with trusted locals, who help you identify possible danger, and avoid confrontation. Brazilians will know when to cross the street – as street kids/urchins are not the same as in Europe.
- Be careful with people who are overly friendly. Tales abound of tourists waking up, with nothing left except their underpants, and Mr Cellphone and Mrs Wallet have taken a ride with that beautiful lady they met last night

www.FromOfficeChairToDeckChair.com

Chapter 8
Due Diligence

"Preparation doesn't assure victory, it assures confidence."
- Amit Kalantri

Due diligence means doing enough background work and investigation, to put yourself at ease. Find out what others have done. Go with a group that you trust.

What references do you have to go ahead with moving and a project?

For example, I checked the currency, and saw that living in Brazil was very cheap when I first went across. In more recent years, the pound has fallen from £1 = 5.5 reals, to £1 = 2.6, although it has come up again to 3.4-3.8 and even 5 reals in recent months. Work out the price of accommodation, and your budget for staying 1 month, 3 months, 6 months. How will you fund this?

Allow for unexpected events, such as losing cards, mobile phone, laptop.

Due diligence means checking the prices that people quote. Speak to others who are already in that country, and allow yourself to understand the costs.

Another example is local property taxes. If you are renting on a temporary basis, you just pay the rent. In some contracts you will be responsible for the service charge, if you take on a longer-term contract. I was even asked to be responsible for the air conditioning unit failure, on a temporary contract. Having a local friend or person to advise on this stops you from being taken for a ride.

Another aspect of renting in Brazil, which never would have occurred to me, is to re-cut a set of keys, and change the most basic lock. The Brazilians do this as a matter of course, in case a previous tenant, or unscrupulous landlord, enters the property and helps themselves to some of your valuables. Changing the lock helps to circumvent this. What insurance is in place in case of loss?

Due diligence also applies to investing in property and other businesses and projects. As a rule, be very careful.

Recently, there was an investment into Brazil, to help in construction of houses, to be sold to people waiting to get their first home, subsidised by the Brazilian government. It was a way to help the poorer classes, and assist a builder in development finance, seemingly run by a law firm in the UK, an escrow facility in the UK, and backed by legal insurance, in case the project went badly. However, what was not disclosed was a family relationship between the lawyer dealing with it, and a member of the consortium in Brazil. There was also a conflict of interest in that they seemed to be dealing with the escrow account, instead of an escrow agent, or Bank.

Consulting another lawyer to check the claims of the first lawyer did not even occur to me, but it will in future.

Due diligence covers checking even what financial and legal people tell you.

The same occurred for an investment abroad, where the company claimed I could do this via my pension. My financial advisor checked with someone independently, who said this was a grey area, and could be subject to the Tax Authorities taking a different view, and thereby put at risk the whole investment.

A good place to start is to find out who is in control of the business, investment or money. If you had to get your money out, do you OWN it, or is it controlled by an intermediary? And even if you do own it, how easy is it to sell or control?

Fulfilling Your Dreams

> *"The biggest adventure you can take is*
> *to live the life of your dreams."*
> - Oprah Winfrey

Remember this process is about fulfilling your dreams. It may not be someone else's so take it for what it is.

Is your dream to have:
- a place by the sea?
- a place in the city, or in the countryside?

Mine was to be in the sun over the winter. Once that was done, it was also to see how to live and give back. It looked very attractive when I was first there, then it became normal. Your dreams may also change and develop once you arrive.

I became aware of a different music, and an easy way of life in the sun. It then became apparent that this was not always open to others, so a few ideas came along to allow that.

Finally, I also found that appreciation goes a long way, to acknowledge what is already working in our lives.

There is a great sketch by Victoria Wood, in which she describes a set of English people sitting in heaven. They are sat there, in the corner, with their arms folded, and flicking through a magazine. One of them turns to her neighbour, and with a disappointed look, she comments: "It's not like it says in the brochure."

I love this story. At times, when I get a bit despondent, or restless, or lonely, or stressed, I remind myself, what am I really complaining about? So living the dream is also about taking on those areas, and seeing the challenges in a different light.

The dream can be about all the little events on the way, the people we meet, the stories we share, the challenges we take on.

What I noticed was that many people had their own version. Find yours. No one can do this for you. And allow yourself to look at it regularly.

I also noticed that sometimes my dreams worked and sometimes they did not, maybe out of my direct control. So getting frustrated or angry did not really make much difference to a situation. At times it may be appropriate to draw a line, but taking a few seconds and asking will this really affect my life, was a good breathing space.

Keeping my dreams at the forefront, I could do with pictures, collages, or a daily journal. There is no single correct way; try and experiment what works for you. Finding someone to partner with, and report a few times a week, helps to keep that alive. A friend, but often a partner who is also working towards fulfilling their dreams, and is open to being asked questions to keep them and you on track.

Allow yourself to have goals, but also be flexible – so that you keep your dream alive. Sometimes people fall short of their first goal, and give up altogether. Planning for this also allows you to carry on, long-term. Some people love to be pushed, others take a softer approach – working this out with your partner, and allowing yourself to play with different aspects may get you different results.

www.FromOfficeChairToDeckChair.com

Asking Advice

> *"Accept what life offers you and try to drink from every cup.*
> *All wines should be tasted; some should only be sipped,*
> *but with others, drink the whole bottle."*
> - Paulo Coelho, Brida

This is crucial when in a different country. You may take things for granted, that you know how to buy things, travel, and sort things out.

One simple example is mobile phones, or cellphones. In the UK, you just go in, buy one on pay as you go, and use it. In Brazil, you have to register with your passport or CPF document. It takes a few minutes, and is worth having done at the store. So buying a chip you go through the same process.

Travelling on the coaches. In the UK, you just buy a ticket, and go on board. In Brazil, you would need a passport or ID, if you are crossing states. In any case, it is good to have some ID, when you are out and about in Brazil, for getting into some clubs etc. Something we do not really think about in the UK (unless you look too young and in your 20's).

The same goes for places to eat: how to use the kilo restaurants, or the buffet service restaurants. Do you weigh the food, or just go to the table? What are the local drinks and delicacies? Is it safe to eat the food they sell on the beach? Check what the locals eat, and from whom they buy.

Even wandering around is different. In the UK you walk and wear what you want. In some parts of Brazil, be aware you do not just wander in to, say, a favela, and take a look around. Notice what the locals do. I spoke with one friend, who was staying with such a rich family in Sao Paulo, that they would take the chauffeur-driven car to drive just 2 blocks instead of walking. I suppose that coming out of those apartments, people were an automatic target.

Also, buying drinks on the street. Find some locals and notice what they do. Be aware of taking out your wallet even to pay on the street.

I would ask locals about some interesting places to visit, and go to places by car, and in a group, which were great fun to visit. There are some groups that meet specifically for this, and have many ex-pat members who join in.

I also found that local people will walk you to where you want to go. I have been accompanied on several 5, 10 or 15 minute walks to help me get to where I needed to go. Lovely.

Ask advice from other tourists and travellers. Learning from their stories can save a lot of time. Notice who is giving the advice, and what experiences they have had. Some experience is spiced with a bit of luck, whichever way that luck falls.

For example, I found that having mosquito repellant plugs was very useful in some parts and worth the small cost. Also, having ear plugs, which are good for the carneval parties if you stand close to the drums and percussion section, but also useful if there are parties at night, or the rubbishmen come to collect from restaurants at 3 am in the morning- yes really!!

In the end, it all helps to begin to build enough knowledge so that you can eventually begin to settle in and take your own cues as to what to do. That decision is up to you.

What Do You Need to Know?

> *"I don't need to know everything;*
> *I just need to know where to find it, when I need it."*

What do you really need to know to make a decision? I would ask myself this at times, and then notice that it often came down to a few questions. You need to figure out yours.

It can be;
- Who is going?
- What is involved?
- What will happen there?
- What happens if I go?
- What happens if I do not go?

So for example, I went out of Rio with some friends, who took me to a place about 2 hours away. They were late, and we drove together. I assumed we would leave to come back at about 1 am,, but it was not until 3 am that we came back. It was pretty far, and I did not bring enough cash with me to take a taxi back.

Eventually we got back, but it was far later, and I remembered to check in future how to get there and back, and what the other options were. At times, I also went with a group, and because we were so many, we piled into a van on the way back, and I managed to get another van back from Copacabana to my place.

Certain customs show up, on a day-to-day basis; that is part of the beauty of moving to another country. Allowing yourself the time to learn, and discover, takes the pressure off, and makes it a source of fun. Brazil may be tropical, but the people can be very formal when it comes to dressing smartly and introducing at social gatherings. It is customary to join in, and quite normal for people to ask in-depth questions about your marital status and family. This is almost a requirement in businesses, before rushing on to talk facts and figures.

Learn how to greet and follow the local customs as much as possible. Brazilians are quite tactile and will often kiss on the cheek, or the men will do a shake of the hand with a pat on the back. Coffee is often served black after lunch or dinner, and do not always expect milk to be available.

In some bakeries or breakfast places, you may need to pay FIRST and then give the receipt to the person who takes your order.

You also need to know what they mean by 'meet at 4 pm'. Is that English time, or Brazilian time (add on 30 minutes to 2 hours here). Getting upset at people for being late leaves them a bit confused. So, organising to meet much earlier allows them to be there when you expect.

Some of what you need to know will only occur once you get to the country: For me, the different social values became apparent. Easy to chat to people, but on the flip side, less easy to make arrangements that people would keep.

I needed to know that this was not Europe, and that it could be obvious to the locals that I was not Brazilian, even when I spoke the language very well. The whole context of trust, and moving around, and fun, is made with subtly different rules.

Who Do You Ask?

As mentioned before, you can ask people:

- Who know about the country, and read a great deal, but have never been there
- Who have been there on holiday
- Who have lived there for a few months, or a few years
- Who have lived there all their lives
- Who live there, but have also lived abroad

Mostly, I would discount people who get their information from the newspapers. It is general, but can be useful to read for yourself.

People who have been there on holiday get a fresh feel of what it is like for tourists. Surprisingly useful, as the short time keeps that initial feeling fresh.

People who have already done what you wish to do make the transition, and each one will have a different story. It is up to you to learn from them. I bear in mind that each one has their own interaction with the people and country.

Local people who live there are up to date, and can at times be a good source. You may be one of the few foreigners they know. So this is quite a good opportunity to shine.

People who live there, and have lived abroad, especially in your own country, can be a godsend. They understand your culture, often speak your language (English in my case) and can relate to your own adventure. They can be sympathetic, so be aware to bring as much acknowledgement as you can in conversation. Brazilians for example are a proud people, and the British have a habit of being self-effacing.. but do not expect other countries to be up for a gentle dig. The people of Rio de Janeiro (cariocas) will often say disparaging things about corruption, or local womanisers, and 'malandro', but if you start to say this to them first, be prepared for a backlash. It is like criticising a person's child. They can say it, but woe betide you if you come out and say that yourself.

There are opportunities to learn from and interact with any of these people. Just be aware that they will have their own experience, and filter how life is through that filter.

For example, other groups bring a different filter:

A religious group may look at carneval as a hedonistic rave, whereas some of the locals might see it as a family, fun event.

Speaking to people in, say, couchsurfing, was a more soft, welcoming culture, akin to the tech people combined with a soft hippie guitar playing culture.

Speaking to businessmen, they would take a different approach, and speak in terms of opportunity, oil contracts, against a background of doing business in Brazil.

Likewise with dancers, who were into the local music, samba and the culture that goes with that.

www.FromOfficeChairToDeckChair.com

Local Agreements, Rentals

If you sign any legal documents, these will need to be translated, unless you waive that, if your language is strong enough to understand. Having a copy in English is always useful in the beginning, for understanding what happens with deposits, and dealing with people who are reputable.

A friend of a friend explained it thus: If you come off the street into a shop, estate agent or lawyer, you are treated like any foreigner, and that can be pot luck. If you come recommended by a friend of theirs, they will TEND to look after you much better, because they can often care more about the friendship than a professional reputation. Just practical advice.

There are sometimes ex-pat groups that can orientate you – just keep your powder dry, and options open when choosing to sign agreements and rentals. Remember that you are in a foreign country.

Keep some agreements short.

It may take more than one visit to a country, to understand the lie of the land. Speaking with someone in human resources who help people to relocate can also save you lots of time, and point you in the right direction.

I remember, on my first visit to Rio, that I moved out of a hotel when I found a place to rent. When it came to signing the contract, I discovered that it had a clause that held me responsible if the air conditioning unit failed! Remember, you can always alter the terms, and negotiate the terms. It seems strange to us, to be responsible, and anything is negotiable. What people are happier with is a tenant who pays, and keeps a place in good order.

There are also taxes like IPTU and service charges, and you will have to clarify who pays these as well.

However, if things do go wrong, take a breath in, and pause. Whereas in Europe it would be quite reasonable for someone to come and fix air conditioning on the day you report it, in Rio, it can take a few days. Why? Who knows... local values; maybe this will change.

Having more than one person look at a contract is a good idea, someone whom you can trust. Find out who has done work and speak with local ex-pats who have good experience.

If you need to sign a contract locally, you may need to bring your passport, or register to have a CPF card, which allows you to buy and sign things in Brazil.

Many things require that you give authority to a lawyer, as you cannot sign these from abroad. So finding someone who can have a power of attorney may be essential for contracts etc.

The same goes for car hire etc. One point, do always keep your credit card on you; do not hand it over, as this leaves it open to being copied and cloned.

www.FromOfficeChairToDeckChair.com

Documentation

"A passport, as I'm sure you know, is a document that one shows to government officials whenever one reaches a border between two countries, so that the official can learn who you are, where you were born, and how you look when photographed unflatteringly."
- Lemony Snicket

Unlike the UK, you may be asked for ID. Have a copy of your passport, your driving licence, or other ID. I take a photocopy as I move around, and have a copy somewhere else should I need to report loss.

Make sure your vaccinations are up to date, and your travel documentation too. You will need to keep your documents on you as you leave the country as well – there is one which shows that you have left within the allotted time of your visit. Should you forget this, it makes re-entering the country a little difficult, but not impossible.

It is also wise to carry a list of people to contact in case of an emergency – should you fall ill. Include name, email, phone number, relationship etc and have more than one.

Leave also an itinerary, or ways for people to contact you from back home, should an emergency occur there. Whatsapp is very useful as it follows your phone, even if you put in a new SIM card.

It may be good to have a copy of your health insurance, and a copy of driving insurance, or travel insurance, all to hand over for emergencies.

If you have dual nationality, it may be useful to travel with documentation which is more neutral.

Documentation for kids, and ID necessary.

Withdrawing money at ATMs should be done with an eye open for safety. Beware of muggers or thieves at ATMs. An anti theft device that is used applies pink ink to the notes of ATM that have been interfered with, or damaged.

If you use such an ATM, and notice pink marks, go to the bank immediately. If this is out of normal business hours, get a bank statement from the ATM showing the withdrawal and take it with the notes to a police station to get a police report.

Using International Organisations the First Time

There are many organisations that can be of value on your travels abroad. From Couchsurfing, to meetup.com, to various business clubs like BNI, and embassies and ex-pat networks. Finding those that can support you, and provide local information is a way forward, but these are evolving each year.

The internet is opening up advice and travel, and keep your options open. If you are a member of an organisation first in your own country, which has places in your destination country, you can be more familiar. I found this useful in BNI and some spiritual practices that I was learning. However, it can also restrict an experience of travelling, so the choice is very much up to you.

Guides to what happens locally can be found in bookstores, along beaches, and by word of mouth. It takes time to find a few people who fit with you. It can be fun to listen to music, go on tours and join in festivities. However, fun does not always equal safe. Notice what locals do, and take your time. We are so used to having a world that works well in Europe, and to be able to

From Office Chair to Deck Chair

travel around with ease, that we assume that most places are safe.

Sometimes your profession may have links into the country, which is a good place to start. People who work, and have a certain standing in the community, will take you in and orientate you best.

Staying with these people and getting a feel for the place.

Some things, like meetup.com for business ideas, depend very much upon who runs them. If it is in a pub, or bar, Brazilians seem to like this. However, some of these, which appear to be business-related, end up looking more like a social or dating meetup, with business only being an excuse.

Chapter 9
A Few Stories

The First Time in Brazil

The first time I arrived, I knew nothing of the language, and thought my Italian would carry me through. It was fun, and I got some of the simple Portuguese, but was surprised that, when I tried speaking in Italian, no one could understand. So a few hours learning Portuguese went a long, long way.

Also, I stayed in hotels and smart areas to begin with. It took time to get used to the climate, the heat, and to avoid going to the beach between 11 am and 4 pm – times when Europeans would naturally go. Eventually, I learned to avoid these times, and to spend that time in air conditioned buildings or restaurants.

Few people spoke English in Rio in those days. The situation has much improved, but do not expect the average Brazilian to speak English. I got by using sign language, and learned not to use the 'OK' sign, which can be confused with another rude gesture in Brazil.

Early on, I was told to try coconut water, and to try some nice music places. Lovely and highly recommended. However, one hotel did recommend some more seedy joints, which seem to be less prevalent with tourism now in Rio.

Taxis would sometimes ask me the best way to get to a destination, I imagine as a ruse to take a longer way around. In those days the pound was very strong, but be aware that some services charge excessively when they see a gringo. Google Maps is a good way to check the fastest route :)

I would go to music places, and quickly be invited to dance, or join in the music. Other tourists were also a source of information, and chance meetings would produce invitations to parties, or even weddings. The attitude was very much come and have fun – though I remember making some friends at the beach. They could not understand that I had a previous appointment (a wedding reception) and so I could not join my new friends to go to a music show on Sugar Loaf mountain.

I kept an eye for what the locals did, ate, and drank, and how they got around. At the time, there was a van service in Rio, which was like a small combi, bus service. Very quick, but an unfortunate incident with American tourists had all of these closed down in Rio. As ever, be aware of the feel of places before you enter. A good guide or Brazilian friend will help you make decisions.

Brazil and Rio were very much a reflection of what I felt. When I felt great, that is what turned up; when I felt judgemental, that is what appeared. And it seemed to be magnified. My conclusion is how life occurs, is that there is no particular country, only my own interaction with the people of that country.

I got to learn to read the street scene many steps ahead, and be on the lookout for groups of kids – and then pop into shops etc, or cross the road .

There was a freedom of exploring the new language, and understanding the many aspects of this curious country. Via the language, many things opened up, which were not available by speaking English alone.

www.FromOfficeChairToDeckChair.com

First Club

My first time at a club was by accident. The local hotel sent me towards a 'seedy' club on the beachfront of Copacabana. On my way there, however, I walked past a buteco, a small bar. People were playing live music, and the audience stood crowded at the entrance. No clapping, just a finger clicking at the end of the song. Why was this? Just to respect the neighbours and not to make too much noise. Alfred, the owner, takes your name, and every time you are handed, or help yourself to a beer, he makes a note against your name. At the end, you pay up and leave. A system of trust that attracts a clientele who act accordingly. Not quite what I had imagined.

On the plane over to Sao Paulo, I was sung to by my fellow passenger, a few lines of "Mas que Nada" a classic of Sergio Mendes and Brasil 66. She recommended I visit Carioca de Gema. So, dutifully, I took a taxi there within a few days of landing in Rio de Janeiro. A lovely samba and live band were playing there, and I remember standing at the bar and watching the music and the people dancing. After a while the locals invited me to dance, and it was very friendly.

Later this became one of my favourite places in Rio. Why? It is covered, the music is good, and there is no queuing for drinks. Just carry on dancing and listening to the music, and the waiters come up to you, with a bucket of beer and drinks to offer to you, and tick off your order on your sheet that you carry. And only once at the end of the evening do you need to queue to pay, and receive a receipt that allows you to leave the club.

It is safer, it is covered area, it has air conditioning and ventilation fans. Some tourists may save a few dollars by drinking on the streets and taking in the music as well. No problem if you are with a crowd of people, but I find the service, and comfort and food options, well worth the few dollars extra.

There are many such clubs to enjoy, from Rio Scenarium, to Bar de Boa, to Lapa 40 graus, and the list goes on.

On another occasion, I met some guys from the USA on a business course, who had been going to clubs which played electronic music, or western music. That is also very good. However, when in a foreign country, something else is available to go to the local sounds and music. Other forms of music there are Forro, sestaneja, samba, chorinho, etc. Having an understanding of the language helps here, and sometimes a visit to a live event stimulates your appetite for learning the language. What are they singing, why are they so happy?

I remember going onto YouTube to find songs, or asking friends what the songs were. I was bought many CDs over the years, with my favourite songs that had been identified at clubs or gatherings of friends, singing at the beach side in bars.

The culture of clubs is also one where dancing, or partner dancing is often the norm. Learning a few steps helps, and many classes are available, which is another way to meet local people.

In many places people sing along to the music, especially at places like Samba Luzia, Clube Renaissance, and the Samba

Schools. Go with a few friends or a group, and share a bucket of drinks on ice. It is a great way to immerse yourself in the culture.

For links to clubs and videos:
www.FromOfficeChairToDeckChair.com

First Christmas

I remember the first Christmas having 2 invitations. One was to a very smart address, where players like Ronaldo were neighbours. The other was a much simpler invitation to a place in the suburbs, to a home with no windows. The first never confirmed, so I found myself in the suburbs, being fed and watered, and receiving a CD of local music. The simplicity and warmth was touching.

Later, I attended many family gatherings of some 10-28 people for Christmas, where siblings, cousins, aunts , uncles, grandparents and parents all stayed or came for Christmas Day.

How to deal with presents? They play a form of Secret Santa, called Amigo Occult. I was given a name, and told to buy a present such as a CD, or something similar. The fun comes when you go up, and give clues as to who will receive the present. Lots of people jump up, trying to lay claim on the present, until finally you give it to the person on your piece of paper. So, the fun is in the game, and the present is secondary. No big deal is made of having to splash out on loads of presents. Children of course are exempt, and are allowed to receive several presents. The other aspect is spending Christmas in a tropical climate. It is hot, and you can go to the beach. Less wine, more beer. A different feel. Note that they often do Christmas Eve, and then hang around on Christmas Day.

I often found that non-Christians took a good dose of Christmas celebrating, putting on a spread, even if they were Jewish or Buddhist, or whatever. No problems celebrating, let us all join in!

A good idea is to take some local Christmas gifts, or decorations, which are hard to find in your host country. Scarcity of something goes down well. This last time, I took some marron glace, from France/Italy which is almost unheard of in Rio.

www.FromOfficeChairToDeckChair.com

Fish Market

Another aspect which is great is to benefit from the local food. In Rio, there is a fish market across in Niteroi. Take a boat over from Praca XV, to Niteroi, and then a 15 minute walk or so, to the fish market (or a short taxi ride, if raining).

Downstairs are all the fish stalls, selling prawns, fish, clams, crab, all in a great display. Now here comes the fun part – find your way around these and then buy enough for your group for a lunch. Go to the back, and climb upstairs, and there is an array of simple restaurants, which for a small fee will cook your main dish and serve it with rice and salad. Then take a few beers and drinks alongside, and you have a fish meal that you have chosen.

Very friendly, and a place to go with a few friends. During the World Cup, a couple at the next table gave us some giant prawns to sample, and ended up swapping facebook details.

This we repeated in other cities, such as Fortaleza, where again, there were fish places facing the sea, and we chose our fish and prawns and settled into a seafood feast, just chosen moments earlier. Simple, fresh and tasty. Nothing fancy, but a lot of fun.

A chance to live like the locals, and be invited by the locals. Do not miss it.

Other places to have fish: on boat tours, the locals would come to the boat at stopping points, with portions of freshly cooked prawns. As a guide, I would see what the captain or regulars ate, or did not eat. Likewise at the beach, what did the local stallholders or massage people eat?

Also to try are places in Alagoa, where you sit in the sea, with a place that serves you drinks and food, from a floating bar or restaurant. Apparently the local fish and seahorses swim up to you, as you are sipping away on your beer. Or places where turtles come to the seashore, such as in Buzios, or where dolphins come in big numbers such as Praia de Pipa (see on youtube).

Other delicacies to try include an amazing selection of sushi: one of the largest Japanese communities outside of Japan is in Sao Paulo. The influence on the rest of Brazil and Rio is in kilo restaurants, sushi bars, and noodle houses.

Try the local markets, which sell local vegetables weekly on the streets. Some, like the ones in Ipanema, or Lapa, have stalls selling fried foods, sweet desserts and a great way to eat quickly, freshly and well. They even serve coconut water to quench your thirst. Many stalls will also offer you a small slice of mango, or melon, to sell their wares. A good way to sample food, but keep an eye on your money, and keep it tucked well into your trousers/shorts at the front. Again, do not walk around with a wad of cash, or be discreet when you take out your money.

Visit to School Graduation for 5 Year Olds

On one visit to Rio, we took a trip to see the graduation of schoolchildren in Copacabana. The school was set up for people in the favela, and to give access to education from an early age. Run by an NGO, and with many volunteers, it was touching to see how they received people.

There were parents there, and a tour of the school, which was for 3-6 year olds, and with volunteer teachers. The children would otherwise not have any access to education. Even at 5 years old, they were given a graduation ceremony, complete with hats and cloaks.

We were given a tour of the school, and got to see the classrooms, and the children preparing together with their mums and teachers. What is quite different in Brazil is that the culture has teachers be much closer and able to hug the children. I mentioned this to a friend, who organised a head teacher visit to Rio, from the UK. He remarked that the UK teachers brought lots of experience , but came away from Rio quite moved. They would recount their experience of observing classes, and well up with emotion. It was as if they had remembered what had brought them into teaching in the first place: the love of people, and of children.

During the ceremony, the 5 year olds sang songs, and parents took pictures and videos. A couple of kids were having an off day, and were facing sideways, instead of to the front, in defiance of something they were upset at. Aw, it was so cute. The headmistress came to thank people, and had to hand over to another teacher, mid-speech, as she was moved by the generosity of people, and the school continuing the dream with which it started.

Speaking with teachers, I realise how lucky we are in the UK, with access to equipment, teachers, safety, and many other facilities, which may not be available in other countries. Added to this, there is hope, as people have access to learning and education, increasingly all over the world. It also reminded me that schools are not just teaching subjects, but are also a place to share common values, and shape many aspects of our beliefs, attitudes and dreams.

I met teachers volunteering, and I met them providing access to keeping kids safe, making sure they do not get pregnant early, and involved in many activities just to allow the kids to go to school. Many parents were from disciplined backgrounds, and this set well for children to learn and develop.

There are instances of projects around Brazil, which provide education. I was invited to visit a school in Rocinha, when I first visited Rio, back in 2003/4. There, Paulo Amendoim (an ex-footballer) invited me to visit a school, which had put over 50 students through school and university, set in the favela.

Dancing at the Paralympics Closing Ceremony

In 2012, London hosted the Olympic and Paralympic games. Due to my dancing with several groups, from Lambada, to Gafiera, to a Samba school in London, I came across invitations to audition for the games. I went to an audition in SE London, one Sunday afternoon, more out of curiosity. So on May 20th, I went down to Kidbrooke, London SE3, to a dance audition. Luckily, although I was at the back of the hall, in about the 8th row, hardly able to see the stage clearly, I was behind one of the Queens of Samba. So I just copied her footwork, and by the time our line came to the front, danced away. The key was to have fun!

Sure enough, a few weeks later, I got the call-up to be part of the Paralympics flag handover show. I had hoped for the Olympics, but in the end, I think we got the better deal.

Rehearsals started towards the end of August, giving us about a month. We turned up at an enormous warehouse, in east London, and were taken through the basic steps and assigned partners and roles. Later we were measured for costumes, and a few rehearsals in we had a dress rehearsal. Fabulous costumes, wigs and colours abounded, and then we were joined by Brazilians from Rio in wheelchairs, and blind ballerinas, etc.

We then had further rehearsals at another venue, with a mock-up of Stratford centre stage. The show involved not only our performance, but also timings and signals to enter the stadium and exit in good time. The choreography had to change a few times to accommodate what looked good and what we could manage as a mix of amateurs and professionals. It was great to be behind the scenes, and appreciate how much preparation was involved.

On the day, we arrived very early, and had one dress rehearsal in the stadium itself, and many hours awaiting our performance. The dancers for Cold Play and other famous groups were adjacent to us. The Brazilians passed the time by picking up a tambourine and singing songs, and having dance-offs and playful jokes about certain dancers. Some of this is available on YouTube, where people shot official behind-the-scenes footage.

The build-up to going out was fabulous, as we were joined in rehearsals by Carlinhos Browne, and famous musicians and actresses and dancers from Brazil. They met most of the dancers, and you could feel the cameraderie. It was great to dance in front of 80,000 people, and an audience of several billion for the closing ceremony of the Paralympics. We swept past people in wheelchairs and spectators on the ground (within a few feet), to dance by the stage. The music and dancers lifted us up, and soon, we had reached the climax with fireworks, we danced off the stage, and then there was hugging and rejoicing and emotional tears. Many people were able to enter the stadium again, and join the final fireworks and meet the athletes. London was truly transformed during the Paralympics. I will always remember the generosity of the Brazilians, in allowing so many non-Brazilians to participate in THEIR flag handover ceremony. A reflection on how they wish the whole world to be part of the love they share.

Chapter 10
Call to Action

What To Do Next

Your next step may be to book your own holiday, or take the plunge. I am available on email, or on my website www.livingalifeyoulove.com. Get details of coaching, workshops, or put into action a plan to make your own reality. Much as we wish to do something, occasionally, we need some impetus to keep us going beyond our mere wishes.

You may wish to take pot luck, and just take off, or you may wish to save yourself lots of time. I am far from the only person who has done this around the world, but there is something to be said for having done this for over a decade. Going back and forth, on my own steam, has opened my eyes to many things.

I would love for you to be able to have this sense of freedom. You may wish to take the plunge, or do it in stages. There is no one solution, but it helps to be as prepared as possible, and do it in a way that suits you.

Look over the notes you have made, earlier in the book.

Your Options
- contact me
- take action
- put in your profile
- set a date, and start dreaming

Ease Your Travel
* contact me to find out different ways to help you in travel

Join Our Facebook Page
* see https://www.facebook.com/fromofficechairtodeckchair

Share Your Stories
* add in to the facebook page, or send me a message

Set Up a Call/Workshop
* skype peterksaunders
  or
  see https://www.facebook.com/fromofficechairtodeckchair
  page

About the Author

Peter has been able to spend his winters in the sun for over a decade. During this time he has been able to expand his experience and apply practical steps to make this work, learning from others along the way.

In sharing his story, he can also call on experience that allows others to do their own version that works for them.

Made in the USA
Charleston, SC
08 November 2015